THIS BOO~ BELONGS TO...

Name:	Age:

Favourite player:

2020/2021

My Predictions...	Actual...
Town's final position:	
Town's top scorer:	
League One winners:	
League One top scorer:	
FA Cup winners:	
EFL Cup winners:	

Contributors: Peter Rogers

A TWOCAN PUBLICATION

©2020. Published by twocan under licence from Ipswich Town FC.

Every effort has been made to ensure the accuracy of information within this publication but the publishers cannot be held responsible for any errors or omissions. Views expressed are those of the authors and do not necessarily represent those of the publishers or the football club. All rights reserved.

ISBN 978-1-913362-29-4

PICTURE CREDITS: Match Day Images, Paul Macro, Action Images and Press Association.

£9

CONTENTS

TOMAS 01
HOLY

POSITION: Goalkeeper   **DOB:** 10/12/1991
COUNTRY: Czech Republic

A popular character with all at Portman Road, giant stopper Tomas Holy shared goalkeeping duties with the on-loan Will Norris in 2019/20 following his summer switch from Gillingham.

The Czech 'keeper made a dramatic penalty save in last season's top-of-the-table clash with Wycombe Wanderers at Portman Road and will be keen to firmly establish himself as the club's first choice goalkeeper in 2020/21.

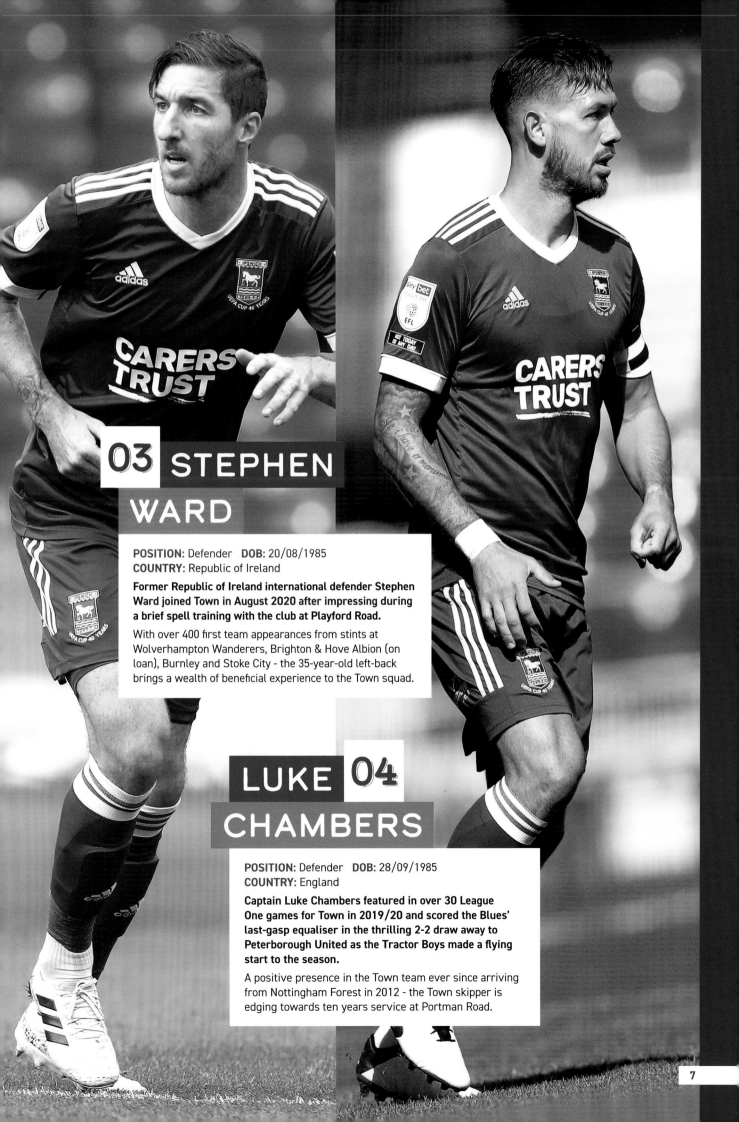

03 STEPHEN WARD

POSITION: Defender **DOB:** 20/08/1985
COUNTRY: Republic of Ireland

Former Republic of Ireland international defender Stephen Ward joined Town in August 2020 after impressing during a brief spell training with the club at Playford Road.

With over 400 first team appearances from stints at Wolverhampton Wanderers, Brighton & Hove Albion (on loan), Burnley and Stoke City - the 35-year-old left-back brings a wealth of beneficial experience to the Town squad.

LUKE 04 CHAMBERS

POSITION: Defender **DOB:** 28/09/1985
COUNTRY: England

Captain Luke Chambers featured in over 30 League One games for Town in 2019/20 and scored the Blues' last-gasp equaliser in the thrilling 2-2 draw away to Peterborough United as the Tractor Boys made a flying start to the season.

A positive presence in the Town team ever since arriving from Nottingham Forest in 2012 - the Town skipper is edging towards ten years service at Portman Road.

ALAN JUDGE

SOCCER SKILLS

Great goalkeepers are an essential ingredient for successful teams in today's game. They have to excel in all areas of the art of 'keeping and Tomas Holy is a great 'keeper that lives up to these expectations.

DISTRIBUTION
THE BASICS OF GOOD THROWING TECHNIQUE

OVERARM THROW

This is best for covering long distances. The body should be in line with the direction of the throw with the weight on the back foot. The ball should be brought forward in a bowling action with the arm straight.

JAVELIN THROW

This throw is made quickly with a low trajectory. The arm is bent for this throw, the ball is held beside the head and the body is in line with the direction of the throw. The arm is brought forward in a pushing movement with the ball being released at the top.

UNDERARM THROW

The ball is released from a crouching position, with a smooth underarm swing.

Throws do not usually travel as far as kicks but the greater speed and accuracy of throwing can make up for the lack of distance and will help the team retain possession. A player receiving a throw must be able to control it early.

> Work hard at distribution and the benefits of this will be seen whenever you are in possession during a match.

EXERCISE ONE

Grab a friend and throw the ball to each other using the various throwing techniques at various distances apart.

EXERCISE TWO

The goalkeeper with the ball uses the various throws to knock another ball off a marker.

EXERCISE THREE

The goalkeepers try to throw the ball through the markers using various throwing techniques.

BOYS OF '78

The year of 1978 will always be a momentous one in the proud history of Ipswich Town Football Club, as Bobby Robson guided the Blues to their first ever FA Cup final appearance and his team brought the famous old trophy back to Suffolk.

Town's quest for cup glory began with a 2-0 win away to Cardiff City at the third round stage. The Blues' reward for their success at Ninian Park was a fourth round tie at home to Fourth Division Hartlepool United whom Town brushed aside 4-1.

Ipswich were grateful to Robin Turner for a late equaliser in their fifth round match at Bristol Rovers. With home advantage in the replay, goals from Mick Mills, Paul Mariner and Clive Woods booked Robson's men a quarter-final match away to Millwall. In the intimidating atmosphere of Millwall's Den, Town turned on the style in the second half with a five-goal showing to reach the semi-final with a 6-1 victory.

Arsenal's Highbury was the venue for the semi-final meeting with West Bromwich Albion where Town made a flying start. They opened the scoring through Brian Talbot after just eight minutes and Mills doubled the lead 12 minutes later. The Baggies reduced the arrears ten minutes from time but John Wark's last-minute goal ended Town's nerves and booked a place in the showpiece final.

On an unforgettable afternoon for all from Suffolk who made the trip to Wembley on Saturday 6 May 1978, a Roger Osborne strike 13 minutes from time secured victory over Arsenal as the cup came to Portman Road.

STAR PERFORMER

PAUL MARINER

Ace striker Paul Mariner was the Blues' leading marksman with seven goals during the triumphant 1977/78 FA Cup campaign.

Mariner got the ball rolling with a second-half brace to see off Second Division Cardiff City in the third round. He notched his third FA Cup goal of the season as Town then eased past Hartlepool United.

His fourth goal of the cup campaign was scored in the 3-0 fifth round replay victory over Bristol Rovers. However, it was at the quarter-final stage he really made his mark on the competition as the England international fired a hat-trick in Town's 6-1 win at Millwall.

JAMES 05 WILSON

POSITION: Defender   **DOB:** 26/02/1989
COUNTRY: Wales

Welsh international defender James Wilson enjoyed an impressive debut season at Portman Road after joining the club in the summer of 2019 following a successful trial period.

He made 31 appearances in Town's 2019/20 campaign and his vast Football League experience is sure to be a major asset for Ipswich again in their bid for success in 2020/21.

LUKE 06 WOOLFENDEN

POSITION: Defender   **DOB:** 21/10/1998
COUNTRY: England

Town fans were given a great boost in the summer of 2020 when Ipswich-born central defender Luke Woolfenden agreed terms on a new long-term contract at Portman Road.

The 2019/20 season saw the cultured defender really make his mark at Portman Road following a successful loan spell with Swindon Town. Comfortable on the ball and swift in the tackle, Woolfenden has all the attributes of the modern defender.

07 GWION EDWARDS

POSITION: Midfielder   **DOB:** 01/03/1993
COUNTRY: Wales

A regular face in the Town team, Gwion Edwards has the ability to operate in midfield, right wing-back or at right-back and his versatility makes him a valued member of the Blues' squad.

The last Town player to score in an East Anglian derby, the Welshman will be looking to add further goals to his name in 2020/21 having netted against Bolton Wanderers and Blackpool last season.

COLE 08 SKUSE

POSITION: Midfielder   **DOB:** 29/03/1986
COUNTRY: England

The 2020/21 season could well see highly-experienced midfielder Cole Skuse hit the 300-game mark for Ipswich Town having made his debut in August 2013 following his move from Bristol City.

A model professional and fantastic role model for the club's younger players, Skuse adds a touch of know-how to the Town team whenever he pulls on the famous blue and white shirt.

TEAM
2020/21

ADULTS

By what mechanism was the League One table decided last season following the Covid-19 pandemic?

1 ANSWER

How many teams in League One for 2020/21 have previously competed in the Premier League?

2 ANSWER

With which club was Ipswich Town manager Paul Lambert once a Champions League winner?

3 ANSWER

Who were the title sponsors of League One before Sky Bet?

4 ANSWER

Prior to moving to the Keepmoat Stadium, where did Doncaster Rovers play their home matches?

5 ANSWER

Can you name the former Premier League striker who is now owner and chairman of a League One club?

6 ANSWER

Of all the 2020/21 League One clubs, who was the most recent winner of the FA Cup?

7 ANSWER

When Luton Town won the League One title in 2018/19, how many points did they amass - 92, 93 or 94?

8 ANSWER

At which League One ground will you find 'The Milton End'?

9 ANSWER

Can you name the striker who left a League One club in the summer of 2020 after scoring over a century of goals for them?

10 ANSWER

16

V KIDS

Challenge your favourite grown-up and find out which of you is the biggest League One brain!
The adults' questions are on the left page and the kids' questions are on the right page.

Which League One club play their home games at Home Park?

1 ANSWER

Who won promotion to League One for 2020/21 via last season's League Two Play-Offs?

2 ANSWER

Which two clubs won automatic promotion from League One last season?

3 ANSWER

Highbury is home to which League One club?

4 ANSWER

Who is the manager of Portsmouth?

5 ANSWER

How many Welsh clubs are competing in League One in 2020/21?

6 ANSWER

Steve Evans is the manager of which League One team?

7 ANSWER

Which League One stadium has the largest capacity?

8 ANSWER

How many League One clubs have the word 'City' in their name?

9 ANSWER

MK Dons' manager Russell Martin played international football for which country?

10 ANSWER

Fill the page with your footy goals and dreams, no matter how big or small, and then start working on how to accomplish them!

We've started you off...

1. Visit Portman Road

2. Complete 50 keepy-uppies

TEDDY BISHOP

1

2

3

4

5

CARERS TRUST

20

ANSWERS ON PAGE 62

6

7

WHO

Can you figure out the identity of all these Ipswich Town stars?

ARE YER?

8

9

10

21

KAYDEN 09
JACKSON

POSITION: Striker **DOB:** 22/02/1994
COUNTRY: England

Former Accrington Stanley striker Kayden Jackson hit the goal trail for Town in 2019/20, scoring eleven league goals while forming an exciting strike partnership with James Norwood.

A pacy and powerful frontman with a neat first touch and eye for goal, Town fans will be hoping Jackson can continue to enhance his growing reputation with another goal-laden season at Portman Road in 2020/21.

JAMES 10
NORWOOD

POSITION: Striker **DOB:** 24/10/1990
COUNTRY: England

Five goals in a four-game spell in the opening month of the 2019/20 season saw striker James Norwood show the Town faithful just what he is capable of.

Signed from Tranmere Rovers in the summer of 2019, a number of niggling injuries interrupted his first season at Portman Road but he still ended the campaign as joint leading scorer alongside eleven-goal strike partner Kayden Jackson.

JON **11**
NOLAN

POSITION: Midfielder   **DOB:** 22/11/1992
COUNTRY: England

Another experienced Football League campaigner, 28-year-old midfielder Jon Nolan joined Ipswich from Shrewsbury Town ahead of the 2018/19 season.

Blessed with a great range of passing skills, Nolan was on target in League One victories over MK Dons and Tranmere Roves last season and will certainly be looking to cement himself a regular place in the Town starting line-up in 2020/21.

JANOI **12**
DONACIEN

POSITION: Defender   **DOB:** 03/11/1993
COUNTRY: St Lucia

The talents of defender Janoi Donacien are no surprise to Town boss Paul Lambert with Donacien beginning his career at Aston Villa during Lambert's time in charge at Villa Park.

Donacien can operate anywhere across the back four and much like teammate Gwion Edwards, his versatility has made him an important member of the Blues' squad. He will be keen to add to his 19 first team outings last season with regular starts in the new campaign.

PREPARING
FOR ACTION

Football matches may well be scheduled for 90 minutes but there are many days of preparation that go into making sure that Paul Lambert's men are at their physical and mental peak when they cross the white line to represent Ipswich Town Football Club.

Like all Football League clubs, the Blues' pre-match planning is meticulous. The manager of course has final say as to who makes his starting line-up but the boss is ably assisted by a backroom staff of coaches, sports scientists, strength and conditioning experts, physiotherapists and nutritionists who all play their part in helping fine tune the players ahead of the manager's team selection.

The majority of the squads' preparations take place at the club's training ground and that all begins when the players report back for pre-season training.

Although the modern-day player has little down-time in terms of maintaining his overall fitness, pre-season really is a vital time for footballers to build themselves up to remain as fit, strong and healthy as possible for the challenging season that awaits.

The pre-season schedule often begins with a series of fitness tests. The results of those tests enables the club's coaching and fitness staff to assess each player's condition and level of fitness to ensure they are given the right work load during the pre-season programme.

When it comes to winning football matches, it is well known that both hard work and practice are two essential ingredients to success. However, in terms of strength and fitness, then rest, recovery and diet also have crucial parts to play in a footballer's wellbeing.

The modern game now sees technology playing its part in training too - prior to beginning their training sessions, the players are provided with a GPS tracking system and heart rate analysis monitors ensuring all that they do in a training session can be measured, monitored and reviewed.

On-pitch training drills and gym work is now enhanced further with players often taking part in yoga and pilates classes while always receiving expert advice in terms of their diet, rest and mental welfare.

JON NOLAN

SOCCER SKILLS
DEFENDING

Defending is an art - not as spectacular as swerving a free kick around the wall into the net or floating a crossfield pass into the path of an oncoming wingback - but nevertheless, just as important. Every successful team has a solid defence and can defend as a team.

Defenders must also master the art of defending one on one...

EXERCISE ONE

Two adjacent 10m x 10m grids have two players, X and Y at the opposite ends of the grids. X plays the ball to Y, who is then allowed to attack defender X with the ball. Y's target is to be able to stop the ball, under control, on the opposite end line. Defender X has to try to stop this happening. Y is encouraged to be direct and run at X with the ball.

KEY FACTORS

1. Do not approach the attacker square on. Adopt a sideways stance which enables rapid forward and backwards movement.

2. Do not dive in. Be patient and wait for your opponent to make a mistake. Always be on your toes.

3. Threaten the ball without actually committing to a tackle. Pretending to tackle can often panic the opponent!

4. Tackle when you are sure you will win it!

EXERCISE TWO

Here the game is progressed to a two v two situation when X1 and X2 play as a team against Y1 and Y2.

The same target is used for this game - the players have to stand on the opposite line with the ball, either by dribbling past their opponents or by passing the ball through them.

The same key factors are relevant here with the addition of two more:

5. Covering your defending partner when he is being attacked.

6. Communication between the two defenders is vital.

If a team can get these points of defending right, throughout the side, they will become very difficult to beat.

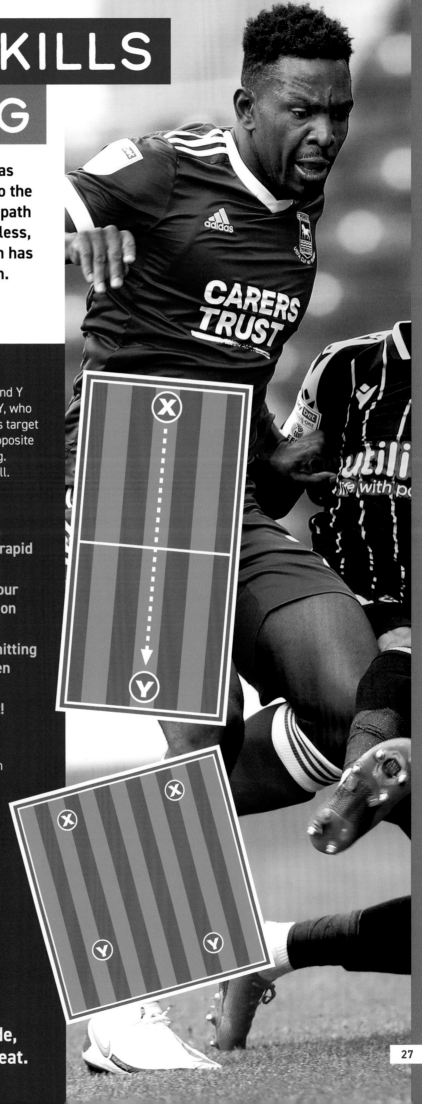

IPSWICH TOWN FOOTBALL CLUB

Take our quick-fire personality test to see where Paul Lambert would utilise your skills in the Town line-up...

WHICH FOOTBALLER

ARE YOU?

1. What is your favourite activity at the park?

a. Leaping around

b. Practicing my heading

c. Lots of non-stop running

d. Scoring goals

2. What is your biggest strength?

a. My height

b. My strength

c. My stamina

d. My speed

3. Which would you rather win?

a. A game of catch

b. A weight lifting contest

c. A long distance run

d. A sprint race

4. You score a goal! How do you celebrate?

a. I turn and punch the air

b. I clench my fist in delight

c. I high-five a teammate

d. I slide on my knees

5. How would the opposition describe you?

a. Hard to beat

b. Determined to succeed

c. All-action

d. Lethal in front of goal

6. What's your favourite move?

a. Springing high to catch under pressure

b. A sliding tackle

c. Playing the perfect through ball

d. Spinning away from my marker

28

7. What is the key to winning a game?

a. Keeping a clean sheet

b. Winning your individual battles

c. Maintaining possession

d. Taking chances that come your way

8. What is your favourite number?

a. One

b. Five

c. Seven

d. Nine

9. How would you describe your style of play?

a. Disciplined

b. Fully committed

c. Relentless

d. Technically gifted

10. What do your teammates call you?

a. Secure

b. Reliable

c. Energetic

d. Mr/Miss goals

MOSTLY As

You would clearly be a safe pair of hands in goal. Watch out Tomas Holy, there's competition here for the No1 shirt!

MOSTLY Bs

Sounds like you are a young Luke Chambers in the making - there could be a role for you in the Town back four...

MOSTLY Cs

You could comfortably take your place in the heart of midfield and help make things tick at Portman Road. Move over Jon Nolan!

MOSTLY Ds

Looks like we have a budding James Norwood on our hands! Who do you fancy partnering in attack?

TEAM 20/21

13 HARRY WRIGHT

POSITION: Goalkeeper **DOB:** 03/11/1998
COUNTRY: England

The son of former Town and England goalkeeper Richard, Harry Wright will be looking to follow in his father's footsteps and break into the Ipswich first team in 2020/21.

Often a star performer for Town's under-23 academy side, Wright has gained useful experience from playing non-league football at East Thurrock and Chelmsford City. The promising shot stopper will now look to battle it out with Adam Przybek to provide cover and competition to Town No1 Tomas Holy.

JACK 14 LANKESTER

POSITION: Striker **DOB:** 19/01/2000
COUNTRY: England

After progressing from the Academy to the first team during the 2018/19 season, boyhood Town fan Jack Lankester was voted the club's Young Player of the Season during his breakthrough campaign.

Sadly after eleven first team appearances a back injury ruled him out of action and he missed the entire 2019/20 campaign. All at Portman Road hope to see Jack back in action in 2020/21 where his undoubted talent would certainly make a positive impression on League One.

TEDDY `15`
BISHOP

POSITION: Midfielder   **DOB:** 15/07/1996
COUNTRY: England

The second half of Town's 2019/20 League One campaign was given a big boost with the return to first team action of skilful midfield playmaker Teddy Bishop on New Year's Day 2020.

Injury had seen the highly-rated Academy graduate sidelined for a lengthy period. The 24-year-old will now be looking to maintain his fitness and really make a positive impression on the club's 2020/21 campaign.

`16` TRISTAN
NYDAM

POSITION: Midfielder   **DOB:** 06/11/1999
COUNTRY: England

England youth international Tristan Nydam suffered a broken ankle in Town's pre-season match at Notts County in July 2019 that subsequently ruled the youngster out of the 2019/20 campaign.

Nydam had looked set for a starting role in the season's opening game at Burton Albion before misfortune struck. With first team experience at Town and north of the border during a loan spell at St Johnstone, the midfielder who can also operate at full back will be looking to impress manager Paul Lambert once the new season gets underway.

BOYS OF '92

After a six-season absence from the top flight, Ipswich Town secured a return to English football's top table as John Lyall's men were crowned Second Division champions in 1991/92.

Town's timing could not have been better, this promotion winning campaign ensured the club would compete in the inaugural Premier League season of 1992/93.

Manager Lyall had promised an exciting brand of attacking football upon his appointment and his team delivered in style in 1991/92. The campaign began with an eventful 3-3 draw away to Bristol Rovers and was followed by home wins over Port Vale and Middlesbrough before Town won 2-1 at Blackburn Rovers to end the opening month as league leaders.

A superb run of form saw Town lose just once in 14 games from mid-January to mid-April – a series of results that left them on the brink of promotion.

Both promotion and the Second Division title were confirmed away to Oxford United on 25 April 1992 when a first-half goal from Gavin Johnson in a 1-1 draw gave Town the all-important point they needed.

Backed by a large travelling contingent at Oxford's old Manor Ground, the Town fans invaded the pitch at full-time to celebrate with their heroes as the club's six-year exile from the top flight came to an end.

Lyall's men were presented with the trophy back at Portman Road on the final day of the season when a crowd of 26,803 saw the party continue with a 3-1 win over Brighton & Hove Albion.

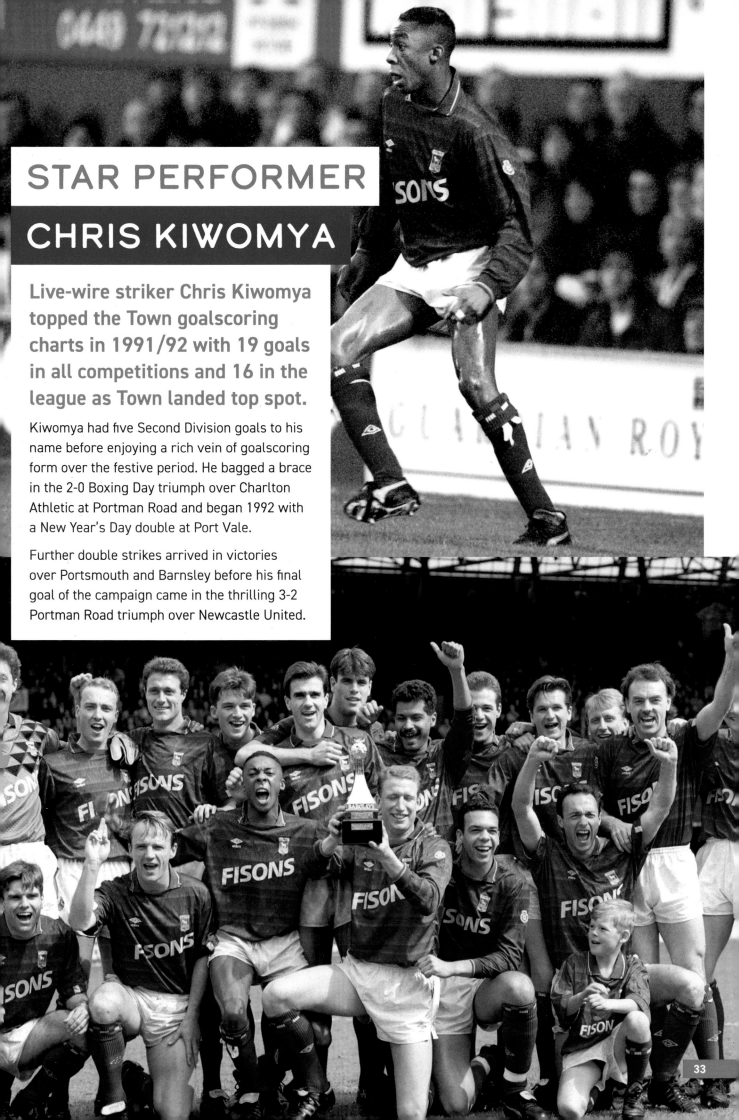

STAR PERFORMER
CHRIS KIWOMYA

Live-wire striker Chris Kiwomya topped the Town goalscoring charts in 1991/92 with 19 goals in all competitions and 16 in the league as Town landed top spot.

Kiwomya had five Second Division goals to his name before enjoying a rich vein of goalscoring form over the festive period. He bagged a brace in the 2-0 Boxing Day triumph over Charlton Athletic at Portman Road and began 1992 with a New Year's Day double at Port Vale.

Further double strikes arrived in victories over Portsmouth and Barnsley before his final goal of the campaign came in the thrilling 3-2 Portman Road triumph over Newcastle United.

COLOUR ARMANDO DOBRA

FREDDIE
SEARS

BOYS OF '81

In the eyes of most Blues' fans the club's 1980/81 side was Ipswich Town's greatest ever team. Bobby Robson's men mounted a serious search for silverware on three fronts in a truly memorable campaign.

Domestically, Town ended the season as First Division runners-up and FA Cup semi-finalists but proceeded to conquer Europe when they were crowned UEFA Cup winners in May 1981.

Inspired by the goals of John Wark en route to the final, Town faced Dutch opposition in the shape of AZ Alkmaar in a two-legged final. A sensational display from Ipswich gave them a 3-0 first leg victory as Robson's side really made home advantage pay.

AZ may have been the runaway champions of the Dutch league but they were no match for an Ipswich side whose Portman Road display ensured they headed out to Amsterdam for the second leg with almost one hand on the trophy.

STAR PERFORMER
JOHN WARK

Having netted a phenomenal 36 goals from midfield in Town's historic 1980/81 campaign, John Wark was voted the PFA Player of the Year.

Wark's outstanding contribution to Town's bid for a league and FA Cup double ended with Town winning the UEFA Cup and finishing as runners-up to Aston Villa in the First Division title race, while their Wembley dream ended at the semi-final stage.

With so many goals and match-winning performances during an unforgettable season, it was of little surprise that his fellow professionals voted Wark their Player of the Year. With Town bidding for trophies on three fronts, Wark played in an incredible 64 matches for Town in 1980/81. Of the 36 goals he scored, a remarkable 14 came in Town's triumphant UEFA Cup run with Wark the competition's top scorer.

Town opened the scoring after 27 minutes when Paul Mariner unleashed a powerful shot that was handled, East German referee Adolf Prokop pointed to the penalty spot and the ultra-reliable John Wark converted from 12 yards.

Town got the second half off to the best possible start as Frans Thijssen doubled their lead just 46 seconds after the re-start. With Portman Road bouncing and the visitors very much on the ropes, Ipswich scored their third goal of the night when Mariner added his name to the scoresheet.

The second leg certainly saw AZ Alkmaar put up a better show on home soil - however nothing was stopping Bobby Robson's Ipswich from conquering Europe and bringing the UEFA Cup to Suffolk. Eric Gates and Wark were on target in the first half in Amsterdam, although AZ did run out 4-2 winners on the night.

With a 5-4 aggregate success, Mick Mills hoisted aloft the UEFA Cup on an unforgettable evening in Amsterdam.

ALAN 18 JUDGE

POSITION: Midfielder   **DOB:** 11/11/1988
COUNTRY: Republic of Ireland

Republic of Ireland international midfielder Alan Judge brings a level of class and finesse to the Town team.

Signed from Brentford in January 2019, he netted his first Town goal with a dramatic late winner in the FA Cup third round replay at Lincoln City in November. His quality was again on show as he scored twice in the 4-1 demolition of Burton Albion at Portman Road in February 2020.

20 FREDDIE SEARS

POSITION: Striker   **DOB:** 27/11/1989
COUNTRY: England

Experienced frontman Freddie Sears was a big miss for Ipswich in the first half of last season. A cruciate ligament injury sustained in February 2019 ruled Sears out of action until he returned for the Boxing Day clash with Gillingham.

He got back on the goal trail with Town's consolation strike in their 2-1 defeat at Blackpool in February. His vast experience and knowledge are sure to be of great benefit to the club as they continue to progress players from the Academy to the first team scene.

FLYNN 21
DOWNES

POSITION: Midfielder **DOB:** 20/01/1999
COUNTRY: England

The real jewel in the crown at Portman Road, Flynn Downes was a star performer throughout the 2019/20 season.

Downes is a tough tackling midfielder who is comfortable in possession and is strong at breaking up opposition play. His all-action box-to-box performances won him many plaudits while making 32 appearances in all competitions last season. The England under-20 international will certainly be one of the first names on the Town teamsheet in 2020/21.

TOTO 22
NSIALA

POSITION: Defender **DOB:** 25/03/1992
COUNTRY: DR Congo

Central defender Toto Nsiala joined Ipswich in the summer of 2018 when Paul Hurst returned to Shrewsbury Town for the services of Nsiala and teammate Jon Nolan.

After suffering an injury in pre-season ahead of the Blues' 2019/20 League One campaign, the powerful and committed defender found first team opportunities limited and joined League One rivals Bolton Wanderers in the January transfer window. Nsiala will be looking to kick-start his Town career in 2020/21.

There are five Blueys hiding in the crowd as Ipswich fans celebrate Town winning the Play-Off final and promotion to the Premier League at Wembley in 2000. Can you find him?

CLASSIC FANTASTIC

ANDRE
DOZZELL

SPOT THE DIFFERENCE

Can you find the eight differences between these two photos?

ANSWERS ON PAGE 62

2020/21

PREMIER LEAGUE

OUR PREDICTION FOR PREMIER LEAGUE WINNERS:

LEICESTER CITY

YOUR PREDICTION:

OUR PREDICTION FOR PREMIER LEAGUE RUNNERS-UP:

LIVERPOOL

YOUR PREDICTION:

CHAMPIONSHIP

OUR PREDICTION FOR CHAMPIONSHIP WINNERS:

WATFORD

YOUR PREDICTION:

OUR PREDICTION FOR CHAMPIONSHIP RUNNERS-UP:

SWANSEA CITY

YOUR PREDICTION:

LEAGUE ONE

OUR PREDICTION FOR LEAGUE ONE WINNERS:
IPSWICH TOWN

YOUR PREDICTION:

OUR PREDICTION FOR LEAGUE ONE RUNNERS-UP:
SUNDERLAND

YOUR PREDICTION:

FA CUP & EFL CUP

OUR PREDICTION FOR FA CUP WINNERS:
MIDDLESBROUGH

YOUR PREDICTION:

OUR PREDICTION FOR EFL CUP WINNERS:
BRIGHTON & HA

YOUR PREDICTION:

PREDICTIONS

ANDRE 23
DOZZELL

POSITION: Midfielder   **DOB:** 02/05/1999
COUNTRY: England

The son of Town great Jason, Andre Dozzell is a graduate of the Town Academy who burst onto the first team scene with a goalscoring debut back in April 2016.

A hugely skilful player, who is blessed with an exceptional range of passing skills, Dozzell was on target in last season's FA Cup meeting with Lincoln City and also featured in ten of Town's League One fixtures.

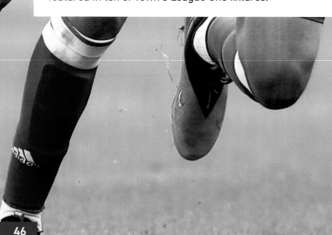

KANE 24
VINCENT-YOUNG

POSITION: Defender   **DOB:** 15/03/1996
COUNTRY: England

Attacking right-back Kane Vincent-Young joined Town in August 2019 from Colchester United and made a flying start to his Portman Road career. He debuted in the 5-0 win away to Bolton Wanderers and was on the scoresheet in consecutive victories over Gillingham and Tranmere Rovers in September.

Injury curtailed his impressive introduction and his absence was a big miss to the team. A fit Vincent-Young will clearly play an important role for Town in 2020/21.

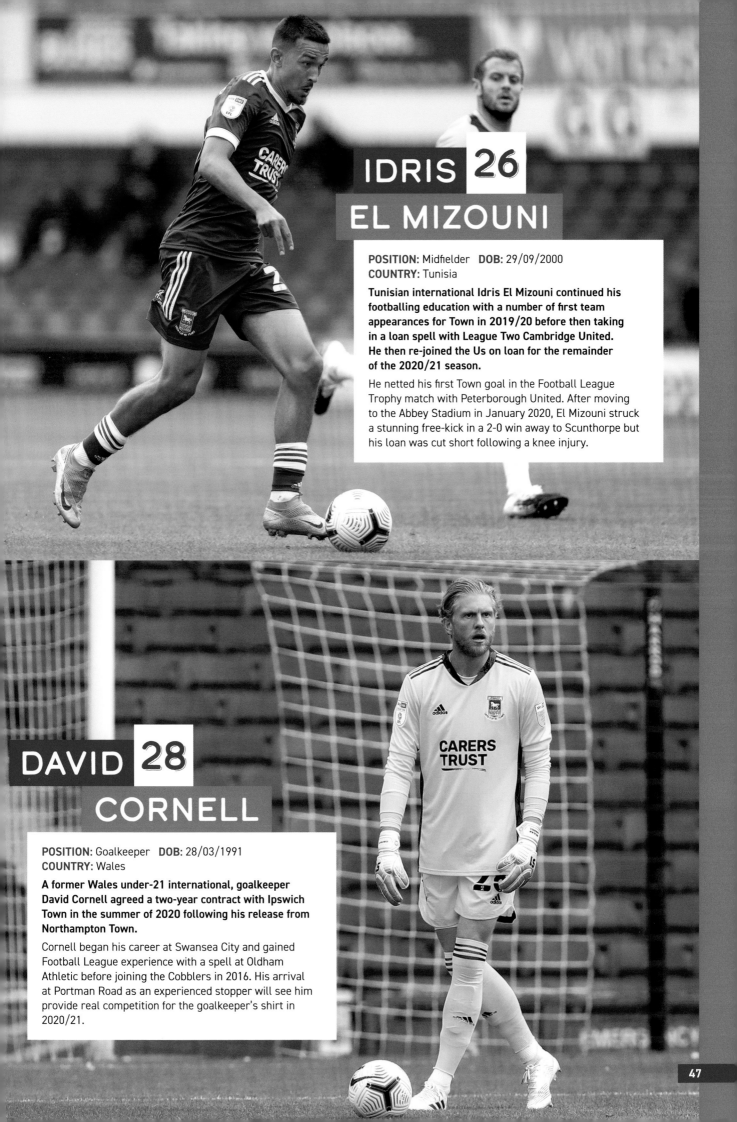

IDRIS 26
EL MIZOUNI

POSITION: Midfielder   **DOB:** 29/09/2000
COUNTRY: Tunisia

Tunisian international Idris El Mizouni continued his footballing education with a number of first team appearances for Town in 2019/20 before then taking in a loan spell with League Two Cambridge United. He then re-joined the Us on loan for the remainder of the 2020/21 season.

He netted his first Town goal in the Football League Trophy match with Peterborough United. After moving to the Abbey Stadium in January 2020, El Mizouni struck a stunning free-kick in a 2-0 win away to Scunthorpe but his loan was cut short following a knee injury.

DAVID 28
CORNELL

POSITION: Goalkeeper   **DOB:** 28/03/1991
COUNTRY: Wales

A former Wales under-21 international, goalkeeper David Cornell agreed a two-year contract with Ipswich Town in the summer of 2020 following his release from Northampton Town.

Cornell began his career at Swansea City and gained Football League experience with a spell at Oldham Athletic before joining the Cobblers in 2016. His arrival at Portman Road as an experienced stopper will see him provide real competition for the goalkeeper's shirt in 2020/21.

LUKE
CHAMBERS

SOCCER SKILLS
CHEST CONTROL

Controlling the ball quickly and with minimum fuss in order to get the ball where you want it, so you can pass or shoot, can be the difference between a good player and a top class player.

EXERCISE ONE

Grab two of your mates to start the exercise. A and C stand 10yds apart and have a ball each, ready to act as servers.

B works first. B must run towards A who serves the ball for B to control with the chest and pass back to A. B then turns, runs to C and repeats the exercise.

Once B has worked for 30 seconds all the players rotate.

KEY FACTORS

1. Look to control the ball as early as possible.
2. Get in line with the ball.
3. Keep eyes on the ball.
4. Relax the body on impact with the ball to cushion it.

EXERCISE TWO

In this exercise there are 5 servers positioned around a 15yd square. At one side of the square there is a goal.

T starts in the middle of the square. S1 serves first, throwing the ball in the air towards T. T must control the ball with the chest and try to shoot past the goalkeeper, as soon as T has shot on goal they must prepare for the next serve from S2.

Once T has received a ball from every server the players rotate positions - the same key factors apply.

Players who can control a ball quickly, putting the ball in a position for a shot or pass, give themselves and their teammates the extra valuable seconds required in today's intense style of play.

In which season did Sunderland last win promotion from the third tier?

11 ANSWER

Ipswich Town were last crowned third tier champions in 1956/57 - true or false?

12 ANSWER

Can you name the two current League One clubs that West Ham captain Mark Noble has played on loan for?

13 ANSWER

Which League One club is famously known for being mentioned in a 1980s advert for the Milk Marketing Board?

14 ANSWER

Which League One club used to play their home matches at the Manor Ground?

15 ANSWER

Other than Peterborough United, which two other clubs has Darren Ferguson managed?

16 ANSWER

At which club did Sunderland manager Phil Parkinson begin his managerial career?

17 ANSWER

From which club did Peterborough United sign striker Mo Eisa?

18 ANSWER

When League One rivals Portsmouth and Plymouth Argyle meet, what is the match known as?

19 ANSWER

From which club have MK Dons loaned striker Carlton Morris for the 2020/21 season?

20 ANSWER

V V KIDS

Challenge your favourite grown-up and find out which of you is the biggest League One brain!
The adults' questions are on the left page and the kids' questions are on the right page.

Who is the manager of Oxford United?

11 ANSWER

Which club play their home matches at the KCOM Stadium?

12 ANSWER

How many 2020/21 League One clubs are based in London?

13 ANSWER

Which League One club's nickname is 'The Imps'?

14 ANSWER

Can you name the League One club that play their home fixtures at London Road?

15 ANSWER

Shrewsbury Town manager Sam Ricketts played international football for which country?

16 ANSWER

What is Burton Albion's nickname?

17 ANSWER

Bristol Rovers are famous for playing in what type of shirts?

18 ANSWER

Which club has the largest ground capacity - Hull City or Doncaster Rovers?

19 ANSWER

Who is the manager of Swindon Town?

20 ANSWER

ANSWERS ON PAGE 62

51

BOYS OF

2000

After three consecutive Play-Off semi-final defeats, Town ended their five-year absence from the top flight and their Play-Off hoodoo with a thrilling 4-2 victory over Barnsley at Wembley in 1999/2000.

After ending the regulation season in third place, Town faced Bolton Wanderers in the Play-Off semi-final and gained revenge for their defeat at the hands of the Trotters at the same stage 12 months earlier.

An eventful Wembley final was only six minutes old when Craig Hignett's shot hit the crossbar before rebounding off of Richard Wright's shoulder and into the net to put the Yorkshire side ahead.

Tony Mowbray headed home Town's 28th-minute equaliser but the Blues faced a major scare on the stroke of half-time when Barsnley were awarded a penalty after Wright had upended Hignett. However, the Ipswich 'keeper redeemed himself by saving Darren Barnard's spot-kick.

Skipper Matt Holland was ever-present in Town's 1999/2000 promotion-winning campaign and ended a memorable season by leading the team to Wembley glory in the Play-Off final.

The all-action Republic of Ireland international midfielder scored ten goals from midfield in the league season – the most vital securing a 1-0 win away to Nottingham Forest in December 1999.

Town's Wembley triumph saw Holland take the mantle of becoming the last club skipper to lift a trophy at the old Wembley stadium. Following the match with Barnsley, work began to demolish the old ground to make way for the new national stadium.

Town made a flying start to the second half and before the hour-mark had taken two huge steps to promotion - Richard Naylor put them in front on 52 minutes and when Marcus Stewart headed home a Jamie Clapham cross after 59 minutes the Town fans began to party.

The champagne was briefly put on ice after Mowbray pulled down Geoff Thomas allowing Hignett to reduce the arrears from the penalty spot 13 minutes from time. With the Tykes pushing hard for an equaliser Town hit them on the break in stoppage time when Martijn Reuser broke free and ran 40 yards before smashing an unforgettable goal past Miller in the Barnsley goal.

There was no way back for Barnsley from there and Town were back up among the big boys as their Play-Off agony finally ended.

TEAM 20/21

30 MYLES KENLOCK

POSITION: Defender   **DOB:** 26/11/1996
COUNTRY: England

Another player to progress through Ipswich's successful youth Academy, defender Myles Kenlock made 17 first team appearances during the Blues' 2019/20 season.

He often found his route to the left-back position blocked by the on-loan Luke Garbutt but will be keen to make that role his own in 2020/21 and help Town mount a push for promotion back to the Championship.

OLI 32 HAWKINS

POSITION: Striker   **DOB:** 08/04/1992
COUNTRY: England

With the rare ability to operate as a centre-forward or as a central defender, 28-year-old Oli Hawkins provides Paul Lambert's squad with a number of options.

His arrival at Portman Road in August 2020 is expected to see him add some additional physical presence to the Town front line. Hawkins was Portsmouth's Wembley shoot-out hero when they defeated Sunderland on penalties in the 2019 Football League Trophy final.

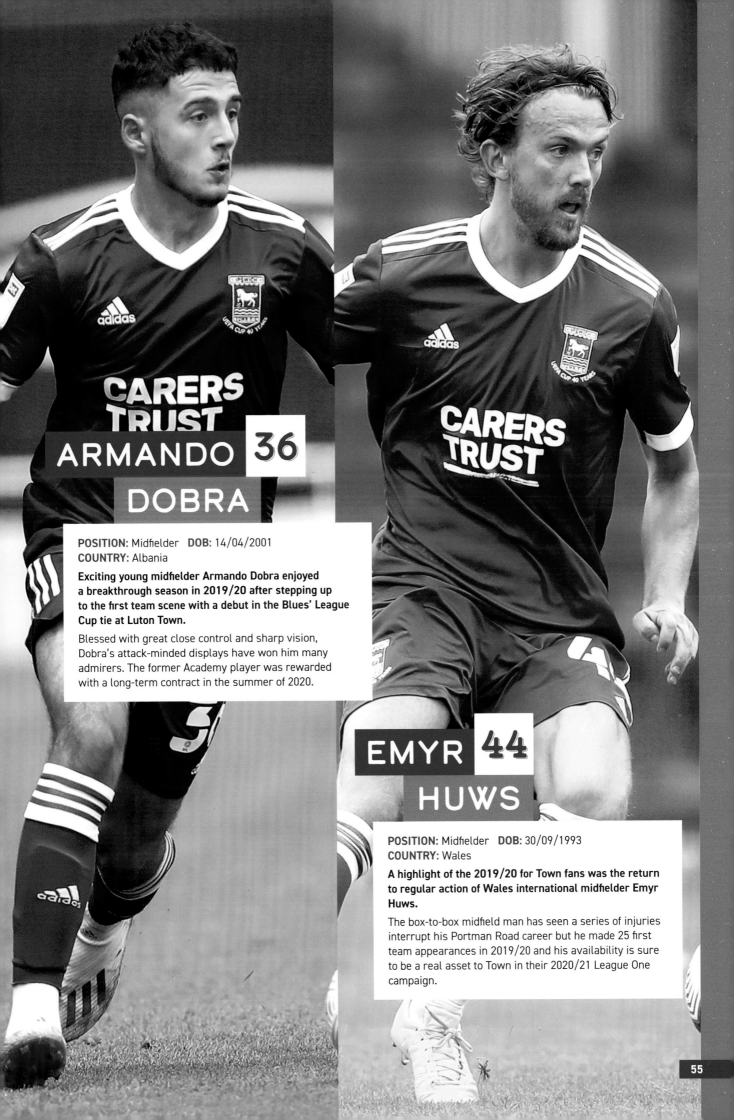

ARMANDO 36 DOBRA

POSITION: Midfielder **DOB:** 14/04/2001
COUNTRY: Albania

Exciting young midfielder Armando Dobra enjoyed a breakthrough season in 2019/20 after stepping up to the first team scene with a debut in the Blues' League Cup tie at Luton Town.

Blessed with great close control and sharp vision, Dobra's attack-minded displays have won him many admirers. The former Academy player was rewarded with a long-term contract in the summer of 2020.

EMYR 44 HUWS

POSITION: Midfielder **DOB:** 30/09/1993
COUNTRY: Wales

A highlight of the 2019/20 for Town fans was the return to regular action of Wales international midfielder Emyr Huws.

The box-to-box midfield man has seen a series of injuries interrupt his Portman Road career but he made 25 first team appearances in 2019/20 and his availability is sure to be a real asset to Town in their 2020/21 League One campaign.

JARGON BUSTER

Here is a list of footy jargon. All but one of the terms are hidden in the grid...

...can you work out which is missing?

All To Play For

Back Of The Net

Bags Of Pace

Big Game Player

Box-To-Box

Class Act

Derby Day

Dinked In

Early Doors

Funny Old Game

Game Of Two Halves

Handbags

Hat-Trick

Hollywood Pass

Keep It Tight

Massive Game

Midfield General

Natural Goalscorer

Row Z

Worldy

```
A S M Z U C E M A G E V I S S A M
V A W T B X O W A C V T S V Y B N
P O I B Y D I N K E D I N B R Q A
R L Q C J K X Z E F M L F J N E T
O G F W K C I R T T A H C S A Z U
E X B H D A V A P N H X G B J E R
T K A L L T O P L A Y F O R D C A
I R C P M E Q M O L R X G H O A L
F L K D N U R A S T T P K Q C P G
U F O N Z Y D I W O M W Y I B F O
N H F W Z O E S B B U N E H L O A
N J T G O B N O D F F X K A D S L
Y Z H S V R X M A G V O R N I G S
O X E A D C L H H G A E U D Z A C
L B N K Q J L D C J N K A B I B O
D D E R B Y D A Y E E S P A L B R
G W T E U O I P G J I O J G S M E
A C I O K I R D Y U X K T S F A R
M H W V Y B L T B P C H F O R R A
E O P C D E E T G E G Q B L P E N
V G C M I H A F M I E K Y V Z G L
H J B F D W A R T X I D H D C T D
L X D M O A S T A S O L G A T C R
V I A Q K Y I H S O D W J H Y A Q
M P F E Z P R G R G U N F M I S G
Z I N Q E J N S L J P I K Z Y S O
D B S E V L A H O W T F O E M A G
E K T X S L T E M X K W U L L I
U S N Q L U W E A B V R S P C O
A Y O R S F I T W Y O T A N B M
H O L L Y W O O D P A S S U T I
```

ANSWERS ON PAGE 62

FLYNN
DOWNES

30 DAY

Day 1
Right let's get started! 10 squats, 25 star jumps, 10 sit-ups - all before school!

Day 2
Make your mum a brew before going out to practice your keepy-uppies

Day 3
10 squats
50 star jumps
10 sit-ups

Day 4
How about swapping the crisps in your lunchbox for an apple?

Day 5
Take a one mile ride on your bike

Day 6
75 star jumps
15 sit-ups
15 press-ups

Day 7
Help clean the car before going out to play headers and volleys with your friends

Day 8
75 star jumps
15 sit-ups
15 press-ups
Before and after school now!

Day 9
Walk to school rather than take the bus

Day 10
Head to the swimming pool for a 30-minute swim

Day 11
100 star jumps
20 sit-ups
20 press-ups
Twice a day now, don't forget!

Day 12
Make sure you trade one of your fizzy drinks for a glass of water today

Day 13
Jog to the shop for your mum... before playing any video games!

Day 14
Give a hand around the house before kicking your ball against the wall 500 times

Day 15
Time to increase those exercises!
25 squats
25 sit-ups
25 press-ups
Before and after school!

Day 16
Take a nice paced two-mile jog today

Day 17
25 squats
150 star jumps
25 press-ups
Remember, before and after school

Day 18
Cycle to school rather than rely on the bus or a lift

Day 19
30 squats
150 star jumps
30 press-ups
Twice a day too!

Day 20
Get out and practice those free-kicks, practice makes perfect remember...

Day 21
Get peddling! Time for a two-mile trip on two wheels today

Day 22
Upping the workload now...
40 squats, 40 sit-ups
40 press-ups
Before and after school!

Day 23
Wave goodbye to the chips - ask for a nice salad for lunch today

Day 24
40 squats
40 sit-ups
40 press-ups
Twice a day, don't forget...

Day 25
Time to get pounding the streets - the jogging is up to three miles today

Day 26
45 star jumps
45 sit-ups
45 press-ups

Day 27
Time to swap those sweets and biscuits for some fruit

Day 28
45 star jumps
45 sit-ups
45 press-ups

Day 29
You're getting fitter and fitter now! Keep up the squats and star jumps plus join an after-school sports club - ideally football!

Day 30
Well done - you made it!
50 squats, 50 sit-ups and 50 press-ups!
These are the core ingredients to your success

CHALLENGE
to improve your all-round footy fitness!

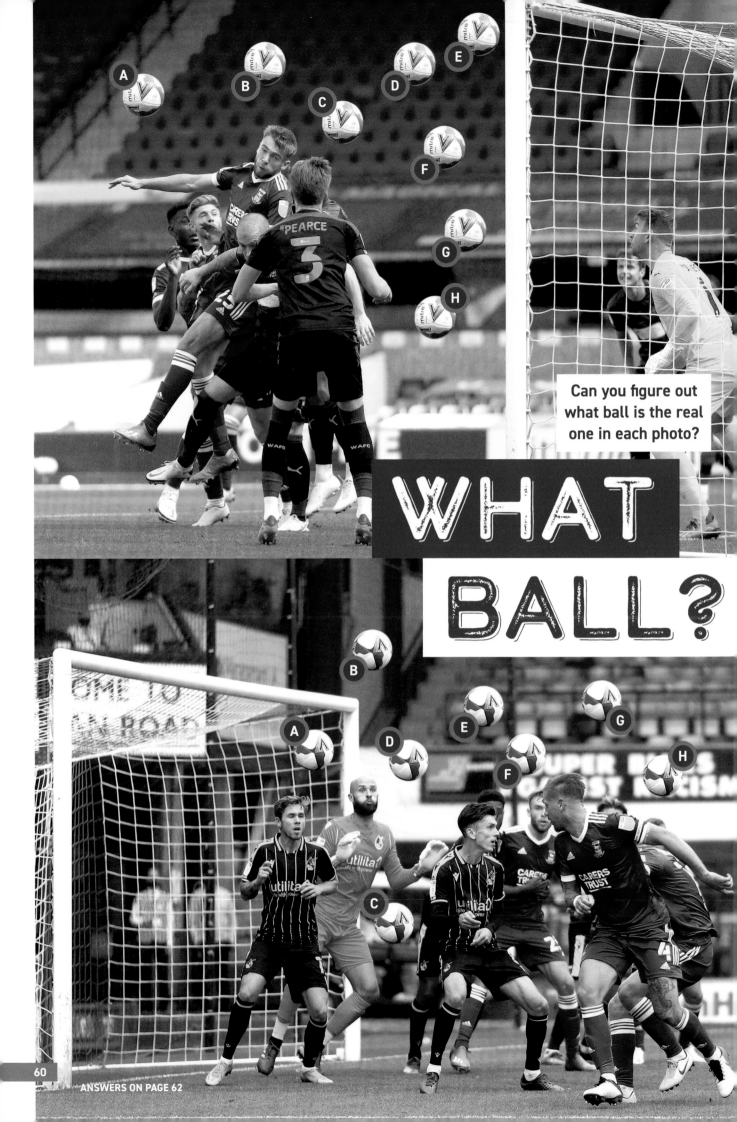

Can you figure out what ball is the real one in each photo?

WHAT BALL?

LUKE WOOLFENDEN

ANSWERS

PAGE 16 · ADULTS V KIDS

Adults

1. Points-per-game. 2. Nine - Blackpool, Charlton Athletic, Hull City, Ipswich Town, Portsmouth, Sunderland, Swindon Town, Wigan Athletic and MK Dons as Wimbledon. 3. Borussia Dortmund. 4. Coca-Cola. 5. Belle Vue. 6. Lee Power - the Swindon chairman formally played for Norwich City in the Premier League. 7. Wigan Athletic in 2013. 8. 94. 9. Fratton Park, Portsmouth. 10. Ian Henderson, Rochdale.

Kids

1. Plymouth Argyle. 2. Northampton Town. 3. Coventry City and Rotherham United. 4. Fleetwood Town. 5. Kenny Jacket. 6. None. 7. Gillingham. 8. Stadium of Light, Sunderland. 9. Two - Hull City and Lincoln City. 10. Scotland.

PAGE 20 · WHO ARE YER?

1. Jon Nolan. 2. Stephen Ward. 3. Teddy Bishop. 4. Myles Kenlock. 5. James Wilson. 6. Luke Chambers. 7. Oliver Hawkins. 8. Flynn Downes. 9. James Norwood. 10. Luke Woolfenden.

PAGE 40
CLASSIC FANTASTIC ➝

PAGE 43
SPOT THE DIFFERENCE ➝

PAGE 50 · ADULTS V KIDS

Adults

11. 1987/88. 12. True. 13. Hull City and Ipswich Town. 14. Accrington Stanley. 15. Oxford United. 16. Preston North End and Doncaster Rovers. 17. Colchester United. 18. Bristol City. 19. The Dockyard Derby. 20. Norwich City.

Kids

11. Karl Robinson. 12. Hull City. 13. Two - AFC Wimbledon and Charlton Athletic. 14. Lincoln City. 15. Peterborough United. 16. Wales. 17. The Brewers. 18. Blue and white quartered shirts. 19. Hull City. 20. Richie Wellen.

PAGE 56 · JARGON BUSTER

Big Game Player

PAGE 60 · WHAT BALL?

TOP: Ball D. **BOTTOM:** Ball E.